150 Affirmations of Faith for Men

Speaking the language of faith will change your life!

RICK PIÑA

Scripture quotations

DEDICATION

To the love of my life, my amazing wife, Isabella, who has always encouraged and inspired me to be the best version of myself. Babe, your unwavering love, support, and belief in me has been a constant source of strength and motivation. This book is dedicated to you with all my love and gratitude. Thank you for "doing life" with me.

CONTENTS

SECTION 1

THE IMPORTANCE OF YOUR WORDS

Setting the stage

I love to tell the story of what Jesus experienced in Mark chapters four and five. Jesus waited 30 years to start a 3.5-year ministry run. During this run, He was busy every day. He did not take Saturdays off. He did whatever the Father led Him to do daily. To make a point of the importance of your words, we will take a brief look at the day captured in the aforementioned chapters.

Mark chapter four starts with Jesus teaching the famous Parable of the Sower. This is "the mother of all parables." Jesus said, "If you cannot understand this parable, then you will not understand any parable."

Jesus went on to share a parable about a lampstand, one about growing seeds, and one about a mustard seed. After the last parable, Jesus was tired. Spiritual ministry can sometimes be physically draining. So Jesus told His disciples to get into a boat. He said, "Let's go to the other side."

What is important about what seems to be a simple statement, like, "Let's go to the other side," is the fact that Jesus only said what He heard his Father say. Jesus only did what He saw (in the Spirit) His Father do. Since Jesus was led by the Father, through the Holy Spirit, in all things, at all times, the statement, "Let's go to the other side," means that Jesus was being led by God the Father to go to the other side of the body of water. This is critical because when you say what you believe the Father is leading you to say, and you say it in faith, without wavering, without a doubt, then all heaven will back up your words. God is not obligated to back up or perform your words, but He will surely back up His. God actively watches over His Word (from heaven) to perform them on this planet (Jeremiah 1:12).

When Jesus got into the boat, He went into the hinder part of the ship. The Bible says that He fell asleep on a pillow. That minor detail gives us a glimpse into how deep Jesus' sleep was. He was by Himself, comfortable, resting, and sleeping well.

While Jesus was sleeping, the boat encountered a severe storm and began to take on water. It got so bad that the disciples (several of whom had spent years on the water) thought they would die. So they woke Jesus up. They said, "Master, don't you care that we are about to die!" Humanly speaking, this seems like a natural response to the situation, but when you live by faith, you are moved by what God says and reveals, not by what you see with your natural eyes. The unseen realm is more real to you than the seen, and you are not moved by sight (see 2 Corinthians 4:18 and 2 Corinthians 5:7).

Jesus lived by faith every moment of every day. He had already seen Himself and His team going over to the other side, which is why he spoke it out loud. He spoke words of faith from a believing heart. But the disciples did not have this level of understanding. They did not understand faith like Jesus did, and they thought Jesus' words were mere statements, not declarations of faith. Since Jesus was living by faith and they were not, He was upset with His team. Jesus said, "Why are you so afraid? Do you still have no faith?"

Jesus was questioning their faith because He had already spoken. Since Jesus only said what He heard the Father say, when Jesus said, "We are going to the side," then no matter what happened, they were going to the other side! I want you to understand how important your words are before you get into the Bible declarations.

Jesus spoke what He believed. Jesus believed what the Father revealed, and He spoke in faith. Jesus had no concerns about getting to the other side because He was in-faith. Come hell or high water, they were going to the other side. The storm did not move Jesus. But since the disciples woke Him up, Jesus used His words again. Jesus spoke to the storm, and the storm stopped! Just like that. The disciples and the other people on the boat were amazed that even the storm, and the sea had to obey Jesus' words!

When Jesus got to the other side, He encountered a demon-possessed man walking around amongst the tombs. So many demons possessed the man that the demons called themselves a legion. Jesus was ready to cast ALL the demons out of him. So how did Jesus do it? You guessed it! He used WORDS again! Jesus said, "Come out of this man, you impure spirit!" With that, with simple words of faith, the demons were cast out of the man and went into a herd of swine. The pigs then ran down into the water and drowned themselves.

Jesus then got back into the boat and went back to the other side. When the team arrived back on the side where they started in the morning, the crowd was still there, waiting for Jesus's return. As Jesus got off the boat, a man broke through the crowd and fell at Jesus' feet. His name was Jairus. He was a ruler of the synagogue. He said, "Master, my daughter is dying. She is at the point of death, but if you would come and lay your hands on her, she shall recover, and she shall live."

Jesus had the power to heal Jairus' daughter from the seashore. He did not have to go to Jairus' house. But that's NOT what Jairus said. Jairus' confession was, "Sir, I need you to come to my house, lay hands on my daughter. And if you come to my house and lay hands on my daughter, she shall recover and she shall live."

If you remember the story of the Centurion and the Centurion's servant, you will see my point. Jesus was so used to being pulled by people to go here and there that when the Roman Centurion approached Jesus about his servant being sick, Jesus was ready to go to the Centurion's house to heal him. But the Roman Centurion surprised Jesus. He said, "No! I don't need you to go. I just need you to say!" He was saying, "Mr. Jesus, I believe your words have authority over sickness. So I need you to speak those words. I don't have authority over sickness because if I did, I would speak to it myself. But since You do, Mr. Jesus, if you speak the word only, my servant will be healed." The Roman Centurion believed in the power of words. Jesus was amazed at his faith. Jesus said, "Go! Your servant is healed." Jesus spoke healing, and the man's servant was healed from that very moment.

Let's go back to Jairus. Jesus could have spoken healing from the seashore, but that's not what Jairus said. See, Jesus will meet you at your level of faith. God will deal with you according to your own confession. You are constantly speaking what you believe in your heart, and God ministers to you based on what you believe and speak.

Since this man said, "Sir, I need you to come to my house and lay hands on my daughter. Then she shall recover. Then she shall live," Jesus had to minister to him according to his own confession. So Jesus says, "Okay, let's go." Jesus left with Jairus, and they started walking to his house. The crowd followed (because church folk are nosey).

As they were going, someone else came into the picture. This time, it was a woman who had her own declaration of faith. She had been bleeding for 12 long years. She had spent all her money on doctors. She did not get any better. She got worse. But since God will deal with you based on your declaration of faith, what she was SAYING is important.

This woman kept saying, "If I can just touch Jesus' garments, I shall be made whole!" That was her confession. That's what she was saying. She was speaking words of faith from a believing heart. There were other people who were touching Jesus. But they didn't have the same confession as this woman. So they were touching Him, and nothing was happening. This woman came and touched Jesus. As soon as she did, the power of God left Jesus's body and healed her. JUST LIKE SHE SAID!

She had been bleeding for 12 years, and she was healed immediately. Why? Because that's what she said! She believed; therefore, she spoke! She spoke what she believed. She kept saying, if I touch him, I shall be made whole. She touched him, and she was made whole. Jesus then had a conversation with the woman. While they spoke, Jairus' daughter died. Someone came up to Jairus and said, "Your daughter is dead. Don't bother Jesus anymore." Basically, the person was saying, "You can tell Jesus to stop. He does not need to come anymore."

Now, what I'm about to say is critical.

What caused Jesus to start moving in the direction of this home? It was Jairus' words. Jairus spoke words of faith, and his words got Jesus to move. He said, "Mr. Jesus, my daughter is dying. She is at the point of death. If you come to my house, you lay hands on her, she shall recover. And she shall live." That was his confession. He spoke what he believed, and the confession was still good. Jesus was still going off of that confession. However, if Jairus said something else, something

AGAINST what He had already spoken, then it could cause Jesus to STOP!

What caused Jesus to move toward the house? Jairus' words. Would could cause Jesus to stop? Jairus' words! If Jairus said to Jesus, "Do not come," then Jesus would have to stop because God will never force Himself on you. If you tell God, "Don't do it," or "It's over," then God won't do it because God will never overrule your own will.

So at that moment, when fear overtook Jairus' heart, there was a danger for Jairus to speak OUT OF FEAR. Thankfully, BEFORE Jairus spoke in fear, Jesus said, "Be not afraid. Just keep on believing!" Basically, Jesus was saying, listen, Jairus, if you can't speak faith, don't say anything. I would rather you keep your mouth shut than speak a negative word. Don't you ever speak a negative word that will CANCEL OUT what you already spoke in faith!

Jairus kept his mouth shut, so Jesus went off the LAST WORD Jairus had spoken and continued to his house. People were mourning and crying over the little girl's death when they got to the house. Jesus said that she was not dead, but just sleeping. The people started to laugh at Jesus. Jesus kicked them out.

At that moment, Jesus could have just spoken to the girl, but again, He couldn't because we must remember what Jairus said. What did Jairus say? He said, "Mr. Jesus, if you would come to my house and lay hands on my daughter, she shall recover and she shall live." So when Jesus was at the house, He was ready to heal her, but He had not touched the girl yet. Since this is where Jairus' level of belief was, Jesus had to physically walk over to the girl and lay His hands on her. So Jesus walked over, laid hands on her, and then spoke to the girl. Jesus spoke words, and the girl came back to life. Jesus ministered to Jairus in accordance with his own confession.

So let's go back and recap. The Roman Centurion got what he said when he spoke words of faith from a believing heart. Jesus ministered to the Army officer in accordance with his confession. Since he believed Jesus didn't have to go, Jesus did not have to go. Since he believed all Jesus had to do was say, Jesus spoke words of healing, and his servant was healed from that very moment.

Jairus believed that Jesus had to go all the way to his house, lay hands on his daughter, then she would recover and live. So Jesus went all the way to his house and laid hands on his daughter. Then she recovered, and she came back to life.

Along the way, the woman with the issue of blood got what she said. She kept saying, "If I touch the hem of his garment, I shall be made whole." She touched the hem of his garment, and she was made whole. I hope you see the importance of your words! You are having what you say. You may not acknowledge it. You may not realize it, but every day you are having what you say your life is manifesting, what you are speaking.

Here are a few things you can learn from what I just shared:

Speaking words of faith does not mean you have to omit the facts. Jairus did not omit the facts.

Being a man/woman of faith who is determined to speak the language of faith does not mean that you have to omit the facts. Jairus spoke the facts first. He explained that his daughter was sick and literally at death's door. Some people (in an attempt to always speak words of faith) refuse to acknowledge the facts (or gravity) of their situation. For example, if sickness has attacked your body, it is alright to admit it and then simply follow up the facts with the truth. Follow up by saying that you are resisting the sickness and in the process of receiving your healing (healing Jesus provided 2,000 years ago) by faith.

You should never allow facts to override your faith.

Immediately after stating the facts, Jairus spoke words of faith. He declared, with his own lips, that his daughter would be healed and that she would live through the hands of Jesus. The truth (God and His Word) is always greater than the facts of this world.

Jairus spoke the language of faith. After speaking what he saw, he spoke what he believed. If you only speak what you see, you will never change what you see! You have to speak what God sees in order to see what God sees in this world!

Your words expose the level of faith in your heart.

Jesus had already healed a centurion's servant without visiting his house. Jesus could have easily SPOKEN healing over Jairus' daughter from the seashore. But Jairus' level of belief was not the same as the Centurion. The Centurion just needed Jesus to SAY it. Jairus need to SEE it. He needed Jesus to go to his house and lay His hands on his daughter for him to believe. That is where his level of belief was. Jesus did not condemn him for it or compare him to the Centurion. Jesus simply met Jairus at his level of belief, and He will do the same for you.

The goal is to speak words of faith from a believing heart.

Jairus did what you and I did when we became Christians. He confessed with his mouth and believed in his heart (Rom 10:9,10). Speaking words you don't believe does nothing. I am providing you with Bible-based affirmations in this book. It is my prayer that you speak the words of faith from a believing heart. If you do, you will have what you say. But if you don't, empty words mean nothing to God because they mean nothing to you!

Good or bad, you will have what you SAY!

When we received Jesus as Lord, the combination of speaking and believing caused God to honor His Word and transfer us from the Kingdom of darkness into the Kingdom of His dear Son. Likewise, the combination of speaking and believing moved Jesus to action in this story. Jesus left the seashore and headed to Jairus' house. When Jesus arrived at the home, the little girl was dead. But that did not move Jesus. He went over, laid hands on her, and she came alive. Why did Jesus do it this way? Jesus could have spoken to the girl as He did to Lazarus, and she would have come alive. But Jesus had to lay hands on her because that is what Jairus SAID! Jesus did exactly what Jairus said!

Even when Jesus was on the way to Jairus' house, there was a woman with an issue of blood. She kept saying, "If I can just but touch Jesus' clothes, I will be healed." Hundreds of people were touching Jesus, and nothing happened. But when she touched Jesus, POWER was released from Jesus' body, and she was healed. Why? Because that is WHAT SHE SAID!

Speaking words of faith from a believing heart got Jairus' daughter raised from the dead. Speaking words of faith from a believing heart got a woman who had her menstrual cycle stuck in the "ON" position for 12 years to stop bleeding. Speaking words of faith from a believing heart got you saved from satan, hell, and the grave. If speaking words of faith from a believing heart saved you from hell, then it can save you from whatever you are facing!

You will have what you SAY when you truly BELIEVE the words you SAY! You cannot fool God with empty words. He sees your heart. Empty words mean nothing. But when you DECLARE what God has DECREED over your life, and you BELIEVE what you are SAYING, it is only a matter of time before you SEE what you SAID in this world!
Here are a few final thoughts on the importance of your words before we get into the affirmations:

- You are speaking words of faith from a believing heart every day. Sometimes the words you believe and speak align with God. So you get what God wants. Sometimes they align with satan. So you get what satan wants. Either way, whether you realize it or not, you are having what you say!

- Your words are exposing to everybody on the outside what's happening on the inside of your heart. Jesus taught us that our mouths speak whatever is in our hearts in abundance. So your words are exposing to everyone the content and quality of your heart.

- Jesus spoke what He believed. He spoke that they were going to the other side. When the storm came, He was not moved. He was sleeping, and He remained asleep. When you truly believe what God reveals to you and speak what you believe, you can have so much peace that you sleep through the storms of life.

- When you do have a storm, and the storm is disturbing you, you can speak to it. Jesus was led to speak to the storm, and the storm obeyed His words. What are you saying to the storms that are disturbing you?

- When you finally understand how important your words are, you get to the point where you NEVER speak a negative word over your life! Your words are truly that important! Jesus said, **"But I tell you that everyone will have to give account on the day of judgment for every empty word they have spoken "**(Matthew 12:36 NIV).

This book is full of Bible-based affirmations. I pray that you declare these over your life from a believing heart and that you have what you say! I also pray that these affirmations teach you what I call "the language of faith." Faith has a language, and this book will help you speak it!

SECTION 2

AFFIRMATIONS OF FAITH FOR FAMILY & CHILDREN

#1

My first ministry is to my family. I am a dedicated husband and father. God has called me to lead my family, and I embrace the grace to do so.

#2

I am my household's pastor, prophet, priest, and king. I don't shun my God-given responsibilities. I pray over my family, I lead them in the way we should go, and I am a living example of what it looks like to submit to God in every area of your life.

#3

As I release my children to school, I declare they are bright, anointed, articulate, and exceptionally gifted. My children can digest, process, comprehend, and understand everything related to their education. God's grace is on them to succeed academically and socially.

#4

Father, when my children have an exam, you give them supernatural recall by Your spirit. They are able to recall everything they studied. The Holy Spirit brings everything back to their remembrance, as they need it, and He gives them the wisdom to understand every question and ascertain the correct answer.

#5

My children excel academically and socially in school because You, Father, are with them every step of the way. Your "super" is on their natural. Your grace is on them to succeed in a way that far exceeds their human ability.

#6

As my children go to school, I declare that their minds are alert, their bodies are awake, and their hearts are open to receive everything they receive as part of their education and social development.

#7

My children are not influenced negatively by the things of this world. My children are the influencers. They are light and salt. They influence the lost to come to Jesus and not the other way around. They resist every negative influence.

#8

My children are leaders and not followers. They do not allow anyone from the ways of this world to cause them to go astray. They walk in the path of righteousness for Your namesake and do not sway from Your path, Father.

#9

I declare that my children's feet are bound to the path you established for them from the foundations of the world, and they will not sway from it to the left or to the right.

#10

I pour into my children the things you have poured into me. I take the life lessons I have learned along the way, and I make time to inculcate them into my children. I teach my children Your Kingdom principles, concepts, and ways.

#11

Great is the peace of my children because they are taught of you, Lord. They are smart, kind, courteous, and respectful. They represent our family and Your Kingdom, Father, in a way that is pleasing in Your sight.

#12

My children are trained in the way that they should go, and when they are old, they will not depart from it. They have too much WORD in them to go astray. The Holy Spirit will bring the WORD to their remembrance, and they will walk with You all the days of their lives.

#13

Because I live the grace life, my children, see an example of your overwhelming goodness, Father, in me. I live as a human example of godliness, diligence, dedication, hard work, humility, and grace.

SECTION 3

AFFIRMATIONS OF FAITH FOR MARRIAGE & RELATIONSHIPS

#14

Since I am the pastor, prophet, priest, and king of my household, I cast vision for my family. God reveals to me what He wants to do with my family, and I communicate/cast that vision effectively. As a result, we all run with it and live together in unity and harmony.

#15

I open an altar in my home, ensuring that my home is a sanctuary and refuge. When my family comes home, we find rest—everyone who comes into my home experiences the love and peace of God.

#16

As a man, I love my wife with all my heart. I also love my family with unconditional love. I can do this because I know God loves me and His love abounds in me.

#17

The grace of God has come to me. Now that it has, I embrace God's grace and allow it to flow through me. I am a conduit of God's grace towards my wife, children, friends, and associates.

#18

Since I am a recipient of God's grace, I am also an extender of God's grace. I am gracious toward others because God is gracious toward me.

#19

I speak life and blessing over my wife and children on a daily basis. My wife and children are healed, healthy, blessed, and prosperous in every area of their lives.

#20

My wife is blessed, and I cover her in prayer. Together, we walk out the vision God has given our family and become an example of God's love, grace, anointing, and favor. The world gets an image of heaven when they look at our marriage.

#21

My wife is equally anointed to walk alongside me. This means that my wife is no less than me in any way. Father, you speak to my wife just like you speak to me. My heart is always open to hearing from You, especially when Your words come through my wife.

#22

My wife believes in me. She believes what You believe about me, Father. The confidence my wife has in me causes me to operate with fearless confidence in this world. I head into every day knowing that my wife has my back and she believes in me and in the God in me!

#23

My wife and I walk together in unity. We can walk together because we agree. There is no discord in my marriage and no division in my household. My marriage is a covenant relationship between me, You, God, and my wife. This is a triple-strand cord that will not be easily broken!

#24

The love of God abounds in my heart towards my wife, my children, and my community. I am a man of God in word, character, and conduct. When people come in contact with me, they come in contact with God!

#25

I set an example for my children in word and deed. When my children look at me, they see Jesus. When my children speak to me, they hear the WORD behind my words and the VOICE behind my voice. They hear the Holy Spirit in and through me.

#26

When my wife and children come in contact with me, they come in contact with God in me. I have died to sin, self, and selfishness to the point where I do not allow my humanity to become a blocker for the divinity that lives in me.

#27

My children are being raised with an example of righteousness because I willingly submit to the grace of God daily. I am a human conduit of the divine.

#28

I communicate with my wife and my children in a way that is kind, caring, prayerful, and careful. I know they are your children, Father, and I will not mistreat them in any way.

#29

My sexual affections are toward my wife and no one else. My wife satisfies my every sexual desire. My marriage bed is undefiled and completely fulfilling.

#30

My wife satisfies me spiritually, emotionally, relationally, and sexually. She is anointed to minister to me in a way that ONLY she can and ONLY she should!

#31

I also satisfy every desire my wife has, physically, emotionally, and soulishly. My wife has no need to go anywhere else to have her needs met because I am anointed to minister to her and vice-versa.

#32

My wife and I walk together in unity. We set our faith in agreement daily. As a result, we are able to bind what is bound in heaven, and loose what is loosed in heaven for each other and our family.

#33

I support my wife, and she supports me. We are each other's biggest fans. We will never be without support because we have one another, and we have you, Father.

#34

I honor the anointing you have placed on my wife. I see her as a woman of God. She is a virtuous woman, and I treat her as such. She is revered by me daily, and our community exalts her continually.

#35

My wife honors me as a mighty man of valor. She submits to me as I submit to You, Father. My wife never has a problem submitting to me because I am continually submitting to You! Not only that but we are also submitted one to another.

#36

My wife and I never go to bed angry. We close the door to every form of discord. We walk in peace, unity, and love. The sun will never go down on any wrath between our marriage covenant. We resolve disagreements quickly and amicably.

#37

Jesus can trust me with his bride, which is the church, because I honor my wife, who is my bride. I treat my bride the way He treats His. Jesus loved the church and gave Himself for it. Therefore, I love my wife, and I continually give myself for her.

#38

My wife and I are patient and kind to one another. We are never envious. We do not boil over with jealousy. We are not boastful or vainglorious. We do not display ourselves haughtily. We are not conceited, arrogant, or inflated with pride. Love abounds in our hearts towards one another!

#39

My wife and I are submitted to one another. This means we do not insist on our own rights or our own way, for we are not self-seeking, touchy, fretful, or resentful. We are always looking for ways to be a blessing to one another.

#40

In my marriage, we do not keep good records of bad things. We are quick to forgive and move forward. We pay no attention to a suffered wrong. We give no space to the enemy and uproot every root of bitterness.

#41

My wife and I can overcome anything and everything that comes our way. We support one another, and as a result, there is nothing we [together] cannot overcome.

#42

My wife and I are ever ready to believe the best of each other. Our hearts and minds are pure toward You, Father, and toward one another. Our hope is fadeless under all circumstances. We endure every challenge without weakening in any way!

#43

Our love never fails - it never fades out, it never becomes obsolete, and it will never come to an end. We purposely and consciously walk in Your love, agape, with one another.

#44

I confess that my life and the life of my wife lovingly express divine truth in all things. We speak truly, deal truly, and live truly. We are engulfed in Your love for us and our love for each other. Your love and grace empower us to walk in integrity every day of our lives.

#45

My wife and I mature in love in every way and in all things. We esteem and delight in one another, forgiving one another readily and freely, as You have forgiven us.

#46

I thank You, Father, in advance, for the endurance and prosperity of our marriage. I declare that our marriage grows stronger each day because it is founded on Your Word and on Your love. Your love never fails. Therefore, the love I have for my wife and the love she has for me NEVER FAILS!

#47

I declare that my wife and I are of the same mind, united in spirit, compassionate and courteous, tenderhearted and humble-minded. We believe God for our welfare, happiness, and protection, but we don't just believe. Our believing is manifested in action; we love and respect each other daily.

#48

Father, thank You that we are a couple of good report. We are successful in everything we set our hands to. We are uncompromisingly righteous by Your grace. We capture human lives for You as fishers of men. As we do this, we are confident that You are the Lord God who teaches us to profit and leads us in the way we should go.

SECTION 4

AFFIRMATIONS OF FAITH FOR BUSINESS OR CAREER

#49

God gives me creative ideas and witty inventions. He gives me insight from above. These ideas cause me to prosper in business and in every area of my life.

#50

When I speak, I speak with the tongue of the learned. God enables me (by His grace) to operate with a level of understanding and articulation that exceeds my education and experience. People are amazed at how I can communicate concepts with clarity and understanding.

#51

The favor of God goes before me like a shield. This favor opens opportunities for me that I would have no other way. This is all part of the unearned grace that is on my life.

#52

God raises up people to use their power, ability, influence, and money, to help me in ways that I cannot help myself. This is an example of the favor of God on my life.

#53

I am anointed, gifted, graced, favored, and exceptional. I am success going somewhere to succeed. But it is not because of my goodness. It is only because of the goodness of God.

#54

God is better to me than I deserve. I experience supernatural favor and grace to the point where goodness and mercy track me down all the days of my life. I am blessed because God is a good God who goes out of His way to bless me!

#55

I am who I am and what I am by the grace of God. I am not a self-made man. I am a God-made man, and God's grace toward me shall not be in vain! I will make the most of every opportunity God favors me to experience.

#56

I am a creative, dynamic, industrious, hard worker. I am diligent, dedicated, and focused in all I put my hands to do. If my hands and my name are on it, then it will succeed because God is with me everywhere I go!

#57

I am a blessed man. I walk not in the counsel of the ungodly. I refuse to stand in the way of sinners. I do not sit in the seat of the scornful. I meditate and medicate on God's Word day and night. I am like a tree that is planted by the rivers of living water. I have a constant supply of what I need to grow. My leaves do not wither, and whatever I put my hands to do prospers.

#58

Everything I put my head, hands, and heart to do is successful by the grace of God. I know I'm not working hard by my own ability, power, or strength. I am not making my own way prosperous. I submit to the grace of God to do what I could never do without God.

#59

The grace of God is all over me. God places His "super" on my "natural," empowering me to do what I can never do without him. I experience The Grace Life daily.

#60

God is ON me, IN me, WITH me, and FOR me. My business succeeds. My career thrives. My endeavors are favored. Contracts and new opportunities are always looking for me, and I have the wisdom to discern which ones to accept and which ones to reject!

SECTION 5

AFFIRMATIONS OF FAITH FOR FINANCES & GIVING

#61

As I open my heart to the NEW LEVELS You have preordained for me to walk in, I openly declare what You have decreed concerning my finances. I have NO FEAR of RUNNING OUT. I have FAITH in RUNNING OVER!

#62

For poverty, Father, You have given me wealth. For sickness, You have given me health. I have an abundant life in Christ Jesus, I walk in the newness of this life, and I experience NEW LEVELS in every time, season, level, and stage of my life!

#63

You make all grace abound towards me so that I will always have all-sufficiency, in all things, at all times. I am able to meet the financial needs of every situation and also GIVE to every good and charitable work.

#64

By God's grace, not only do I have what I need for the operating expenses of my family, but I am in a position to operate in excess, overflow, and abundance. With this excess, I fund Kingdom projects all over the world.

#65

There was a time in my life when I experienced lack. But those days are over. The God of overflow has made money part of our ministry. God gives us money with a mission and prosperity with a purpose!

#66

I sow bountifully; therefore, I reap bountifully. I give cheerfully, and God freely ministers to me the seed for sowing. Not only that, but God multiplies the seed as I sow it.

#67

There is no lack in my household. You, Father, supply all our needs according to Your riches in glory by Christ Jesus. Father, You are my source and supply! I look to no other source. You will never run out. Your blessing makes Your children rich and adds no sorrow with it.

#68

I have given, and I continually give. Therefore, You give unto me: good measure, pressed down, shaken together, and running over. You cause men to give into my bosom. With the same measure that I give, it is given unto me.

#69

You take pleasure in the prosperity of Your servant. I am in Christ, and Christ is in me. Because of Jesus, the Blessing of Abraham is on me. Abraham's blessings are mine!

#70

I walk in the Blessing of Jesus, which is a Spiritual blessing. And I walk in the Blessing of Abraham, which is a natural blessing. I am blessed spiritually and naturally. I live in the spirit, and You make sure I have MORE THAN ENOUGH to meet the natural needs of this present world.

#71

I am blessed in the city, blessed in the field, blessed coming in, and blessed going out. My health, relationships, businesses, bank accounts, investments, and properties all flourish. I am prosperous in every area of my life.

#72

On this planet, I am seen as the provider of my household. But ultimately, God, You are my provider. My God is my source. Therefore, I do not take on any pressure to perform. I open my heart to God's grace, and it causes me to prosper in every way.

#73

My wife and I are abundantly supplied, with every need met, in the Name of Jesus. We have obtained the favor of the Lord. The will of God is done in our lives daily. The same is said of our children and children's children.

#74

In this season, I will give more than I have ever given, and I will do it with a cheerful heart! My heart is in my giving. I take pleasure in sowing seeds into God's Kingdom. Funding God's projects is part of my earthly assignment.

#75

My wife and I have the heart to give. We sow into projects that advance God's Kingdom all over this world. We live to honor the Lord, and we take pleasure in advancing His Kingdom!

#76

My wife and I see giving as an act of worship. We worship the Lord in song, dance, and giving. We do this consistently and in a way that is ever-increasing. The more God gives us, the more we sow into His Kingdom.

#77

My wife and I live to give. Since our heart is in our giving, God causes us to increase in every area and facet of our lives to the point where we leave an inheritance for our children and children's children.

#78

The debt cycle has been broken over my household! We will never lack a thing! We give on a NEW LEVEL, and we REAP on LEVELS upon LEVELS in this season and in every season of our lives!

SECTION 6

AFFIRMATIONS OF FAITH FOR DIVINE HEALTH & HEALING

#79

As the Pastor of my home, I come up against every sickness, illness, disease, bacteria, virus, or germ that attempts to attack my family. I release the power of God over it, and it must flee from us!

#80

As the Pastor of my home, I speak life and blessing over the physical bodies of my family members. I declare that if any sickness, virus, germ, bacteria, or disease attaches itself to our bodies, it must die instantly.

#81

I plead the blood of Jesus over the physical bodies of my family members. I declare that every system of our bodies (every organ, all the blood, all of our joints) will function in the perfection in which Christ Jesus created them to function.

#82

My family will live long and strong and declare the works of the Lord. We will not leave this planet until we have accomplished ALL we are destined to do. We live purpose-filled lives and are healthy as we walk out our purpose.

#83

In the Name of Jesus, I believe I am healed according to 1 Peter 2:24. Your Word teaches me that Jesus Himself took my infirmities and bore my sicknesses. Therefore, with great boldness and confidence, I stand on the authority of Your Word and declare that I am redeemed from the curse of sickness. I refuse to tolerate its symptoms.

#84

Satan, I speak to you in Jesus' Name, and I proclaim that your principalities, powers, rulers of the darkness of this world, and spiritual wickedness in high places are bound from operating against me in any way. I am loosed from your assignment. I am the property of the Almighty God, and I give you no place in me. I dwell in the secret place of the Most-High God, and I abide under the shadow of the Almighty, whose power no foe can withstand.

#85

Father, Your Word says that the angel of the Lord encamps round about me and delivers me from every evil work. No evil shall befall me; no plague or calamity shall come near my dwelling. Your Word abides in me, and it is life and medicine to my flesh. The Law of the Spirit of life in Christ Jesus operates in me, making me free from the Law of sin and death.

#86

I hold fast to the confession of Your Word. I stand steadfast and unmovable. I know health and healing are mine now, in Jesus' Name. I believe and receive the health and healing You, Father, provided to me through the finished work of my Lord Jesus Christ!

#87

Jesus healed out of a heart of compassion, and when He died for me, He redeemed me from the curse of sickness and disease. He conquered the devil in his own domain and took back all the devil's authority. Jesus has now given that authority back to those who believe. I exercise that authority when I speak the Name of Jesus by faith! In His name, I release health and healing over my family.

#88

I know it is God's will to heal me! I have a covenant with God, including my total healing. There is nothing terminal about any disease that attaches itself to my body or the bodies of my household. God's Word says Jesus' stripes healed me, so I am healed, and no weapons formed against me shall prosper! The Word is sown into my heart, I receive it, and I reap a harvest of healing.

#89

Even if I feel weak, I don't give in to those feelings. When I am weak, the power of Christ rests upon me, making me strong! I believe God's Word is truth. The Word says that God heals me from all my infirmities. I abide in this Word, which brings life to my body and health/healing to all my flesh.

#90

I am healthy inside and out. I am free from unforgiveness and strife. I refuse to harbor bitterness in my heart. I know unforgiveness can open the door to disease in my life. So I walk in Your love, empowered by Your Spirit! I am quick to forgive, I never allow a root of bitterness to grow in my heart, and I enjoy the liberty that comes from having clean hands and a pure heart.

#91

I have abundant life through Your Word, Father, and Your healing power flows to every organ, cell, tissue, and joint in my body, bringing life and health. If sickness or disease touches my body or the bodies of my family members, it must die instantly because I am redeemed from the curse of the Law. THE CURSE has NO POWER over me or anyone in my household.

#92

I have control of my appetite; it does not have control of me. I eat healthy foods, drink enough liquids, exercise to remain strong, stretch to remain flexible, and maintain an attitude that honors the physical body You provided to me, Father. I only get ONE BODY, so I will honor it and take care of it.

#93

Father, I am submitted to You in all ways, including my physical body. I watch what goes in my mouth. I get sufficient sleep and rest. I resist negative stress, which can take a physical toll on my body. I am healthy inside and out!

#94

So, I will not die because I am sick. I will not die because I am old. I will only die when I am DONE! I will not die until I get OUT OF ME everything my God placed IN ME while I am in the land of the living!

#95

I am physically healthy. Until I complete my assignment on this planet, no sickness, disease, virus, germ, bacteria, or demonic spirit can stop my body! I am also spiritually healthy. No devil, demon, or demonic force has any power over me. No hex, vex, work of sorcery, or spell can touch me. No dark power has any power over me.

#96

Father, since I am not on this planet doing my own thing -- and I am here representing You,

Father, doing Your will -- no weapon formed against me shall prosper. If the attack looks like it is working, the battle is not over. You will turn it around for my good! I know GREATER IS COMING FOR ME!

SECTION 7

AFFIRMATIONS OF FAITH FOR MY RELATIONSHIP WITH GOD

#97

I have the wisdom to lead my family in the way they should go. Even my adult children come to me for guidance and understanding. I receive insight and wisdom from above. As a result, I cast a vision for my family, and they look to me for strength and wisdom. They follow me as I follow You, Father!

#98

My God is able to give me perfect wisdom and supernatural understanding. The Father united me with Christ Jesus, and for my benefit, He made Jesus to become wisdom itself. This means I have access to wisdom from above. Jesus causes me to operate with a level of wisdom that exceeds my education and experience.

#99

God floods my eyes with light so that I may know the hope of my calling and the exceeding great riches that God has placed in heavenly places in Christ Jesus, towards everyone who believes. This light gives me wisdom that causes me and my household to prosper daily!

#100

I am a believer and not a doubter. I walk by faith and not by fear. Fear has no power over me. I live my life with fearless confidence daily because my confidence is rooted and grounded in God.

#101

I am not religious, and I have been delivered from performance-based religion. I'm not relying on my performance to make me right before God. Jesus made me right.

#102

I am righteous right now! I am not righteous because of what I do or because of what I fail to do. I am only righteous because of what Jesus did. I accept His righteousness, and I embrace it NOW!

#103

I am the righteousness of God by faith. God took my sin and put it on Jesus. God took Jesus' righteousness and put it on me. This is a great exchange. I traded places with Jesus. He

took my place on the cross, and I now take His
place on the earth. As Jesus is, so am I in this
world.

#104

Because I know I am the righteousness of God,
and I am not living my life based on my
performance. I willingly die to self and yield to
you, Father, for you to do, within and through
me, whatever You desire.

#105

I am not on this planet to do my will. I am
here to do the will of the Father who sent me,
and I perform His bidding all the days of my
life. God's love and light flow through me
daily.

#106

I can declare what Jesus decreed: "If you have
seen me, you've seen the Father." Like Jesus, I
say, "I am one with you, God, and you are one
with me. When people see me, they will see
You because You live in me!"

#107

The words I speak are not my words. The work I perform is not my work. It is the Father who lives in me. He gives me the words, and He performs at work.

SECTION 8

AFFIRMATIONS OF FAITH FOR WALKING IN DIVINE PURPOSE

#108

I declare that my family will accomplish everything You sent us to this planet to accomplish, Father. We will not die because we are sick. We will not die because we are old. We will not die because of some freak accident. We are purpose-driven in all things, and we will only die when we are done!

#109

When the day comes that we have finished our race and accomplished everything you sent us to this planet to accomplish, every one of my family members will give up the ghost. At that point, we will get to graduate from earth to glory, from time to eternity, because we have completed our assignment.

#110

I manage time and change correctly. I do not waste time, and I am not overwhelmed by change. I have the grace to make the most of every time and season, and I also have the grace to manage and handle everything (good and challenging) that comes my way.

#111

In me, my family has an example of what it looks like for a human to be submitted to the divine. Since my humanity is submitted to my divinity, I am walking around this planet on a daily basis, allowing my God to work ON me, IN me, WITH me, and FOR me!

#112

I am who God says I am, I will do what God says I can do, and I will accomplish what God sent me to this planet to accomplish before I die. This is my declaration, and I speak it all the time!

#113

My wife has discovered her divine purpose. I support her in her pursuit of it. There is no competitive jealousy between us. I support her, and she supports me. Together, we get to become the man and woman You destined us to be, and we complete our divine assignments before we die.

#114

In addition to our individual assignments, my wife and I know there are some things we are called to do together. There are things You called US to do, and we will get them DONE before we die. We walk together in unity and with a unified purpose. The results are supernatural and world-changing!

#115

My wife and I are world-changers because we walk in divine purpose all the days of our lives. We dwell in Your presence, we understand our individual and combined purpose, and we are completely purposeful in all we do. As a result, the world gets to see what heaven looks like as we experience heaven-on-earth!

#116

My wife and I support our children. We know they are ultimately YOUR children. You sent them to this planet at just the right time. You gave them a purpose and grace for the purpose. You gave them both grace and purpose, in Christ Jesus, before the beginning of time. We are graced to parent our children and usher them into their divine purpose. They will become the men/women they are destined to be, and they will leave a mark in this world that will not easily be erased!

SECTION 9

AFFIRMATIONS OF FAITH FOR SOUL PROSPERITY

#117

I don't worry about anything. Instead, I pray about everything. I go to God in prayer, He hears my prayers, and as a result, the peace of God, which passes all understanding, pulls guard duty around my heart and mind.

#118

Because I meditate and medicate on God's Word day and night, I believe what God believes about me. This enables me to live with supernatural peace and confidence.

#119

By taking control of my thoughts, I take control of my life. I tell my mind what to meditate on. I direct my will to make decisions that line up with Your purpose for me. My mind, emotions, and will are all aligned with God and His purpose for my life.

#120

I no longer allow uncontrolled thoughts to lead to uncontrolled feelings. I don't live by feelings. I live by faith. I focus my thoughts on my God and His Word! In turn, my feelings amplify my thoughts, and I feel the way God wants me to feel in every moment.

#121
I enter every day declaring that my mind is alert, my body is awake, my thoughts are sharp, and in check, my focus is clear, my purpose is before me, my God is with me, and success is inevitable!

#122
I refuse to allow negative thoughts to run roughshod over my life. I will never again allow feelings to control me. From this day forward, I tell my feelings how to feel. I never allow myself to delve into despair or depression. By taking control of my thoughts, I take control of my feelings.

#123
I take control of every negative thought. I know which thoughts to receive and which ones to reject. I receive the thoughts that come from God. I reject the ones that come from satan.

#124

Although I walk in the flesh, I do not war after the flesh. I pull down every negative thought, image, and stronghold. I bring every wayward thought into subjection, and I bring all my thoughts under the obedience of Christ.

#125

God is on my side because I am on His. As a result, I have peace in my heart, and fear has no power over me. I overcome evil with good and am overwhelmed with God's goodness daily.

#126

I have peace and confidence on the inside of me. This supernatural peace and confidence are so strong that I am not moved by what happens on the outside! I can be surrounded by chaos and still have peace.

#127

I see myself the way God sees me. I believe what God believes about me. I look in the mirror, and I love what I see. I was created in the image and likeness of my God. As Jesus is, so am I in this world. With this mindset, I am able to walk with God daily and enjoy perfect peace.

#128

I trust God with my whole heart. As a result, He gives me perfect peace. Fear has no power over me. I have learned how to enter into God's rest daily. There is a place called "REST," and it is where I dwell!

SECTION 10

AFFIRMATIONS OF FAITH FOR OVERALL SUCCESS, WISDOM & FAVOR

#129

I make my ears attentive to skillful and Godly wisdom, inclining and directing my heart and mind to Godly understanding. As I hear from my God, I apply what I hear. My learning turns into living and I experience divine success as a result.

#130

I apply all of my power to the quest for wisdom and understanding. My heart is OPEN to You, Father, and I hear from You on a daily basis. I am led by Your Spirit in all things, and I apply Your wisdom, even when it makes no sense to me (in the natural). Living this way causes me to experience Your best.

#131

I live considerately with my wife, with an intelligent recognition of our marriage relationship. I honor my wife as the woman You have called her to be. Together, we are joint-heirs to the throne with Jesus. As joint-heirs, we walk in unity so that our prayers will not be hindered or cut off.

#132

Father, I come to you in the name of Your dear Son. Jesus is the Apostle and High Priest over my profession, and what I profess is the Word of God concerning favor over my life. Your favor goes before me like a shield.

#133

Like Joseph, I prosper in every place and in every situation I am in, because You, Lord, are always with me. I experience preferential treatment everywhere I go. You cause people to go out of their way to help me!

#134

I declare that I am blessed and highly favored in every area of my life. The favor of God goes before me continually, and it quenches all fear. The fear of failure has no power over me. I expect to succeed and experience supernatural progress.

#135

I am not a self-made man. I am a God-made man. I enjoy divine favor daily. Favor can do more in a minute than labor can do in a lifetime. I receive countless things I did not earn! God's grace and favor cause me to experience unearned and supernatural success daily and throughout each day.

#136

I associate with those who are wise, blessed, and highly favored. What is on them rubs off on me and vice-versa. Wisdom is transferred by association. My relationships help me to experience an increase in every area of my life.

#137

You, Lord, made Jesus to be sin for me, that I might be made the righteousness of God in Him. As the righteousness of God, I declare that I am highly favored in Your sight. I experience Your best because of Jesus!

#138

I operate in integrity and seek to do good in Your sight daily; as a result, I obtain favor from You, God. Doors are open for me that no man can close, and doors are closed that no man can open.

#139

I walk in Your Word daily, Father. Your Word
is the ruler by which I judge every decision.
Your wisdom is the guide for my life. By
seeking Your wisdom and not my own, I
receive Your favor in every area of my life.

#140

Your favor is life, and it endures for a lifetime.
My enemies cannot triumph over me because
of Your favor upon my life. You, Father,
surround and protect me with favor like a
shield. This shield is all over me, and it goes
before me, setting the conditions for divine
success!

#141

I will not allow any corrupt communication to
proceed out of my mouth that will cancel out
my profession of faith. My belly is satisfied
with the fruit of my mouth, and I only speak
that which is good, full of grace, edifying to
others and strength unto my bones.

#142

God is ON me, IN me, WITH me, and FOR me. There is no way I can lose. If God is for me, he is more than the entire world against me.

#143

Everything I put my hands to do prospers because God is with me everywhere I go. God's presence brings with it His peace, power, protection, and prosperity!

#144

I meditate and meditate on God's word day and night, I keep God's Word continually on my lips, and I turn my meditation into movement. I launch out to do what God placed in my heart. Living this way, I make my own way prosperous, and I have good success by the grace of God.

#145

I am bold, confident, and very courageous because I know the Lord is with me whithersoever I go! I am never hopeless because I am never helpless!

#146

Lord, I know you will never leave me, forsake me, nor turn your back on me. You will never relax the grip You have on me, not to any degree. Understanding this, I live with a level of confidence that is supernatural.

#147

I declare that You are raising up people who will use their power, their ability, their influence, and their money to help me in ways I cannot help myself. You do this for me freely, because You love me and because You are dedicated to the plans You made for me before the world began.

#148

I will never be without the favor of God for the rest of my life. Your favor rests upon me richly. Divine favor profusely abounds in me, on me, and for me! I am a part of the generation that is experiencing God's favor immeasurably, limitlessly, and surpassingly.

#149

Because of Your favor, Father, I experience supernatural increase, consistent promotion, complete restoration, full restitution, overwhelming honor, increases in assets, supernatural victories, earthly recognition, positions of prominence, preferential treatment, petitions granted, policies and rules changed, and battles won in which I do not have to fight. All of this comes by Your grace, and I rest in Your finished work!

#150

My God is a God of progression and not regression. I walk with God, and He walks with me. As a result, my progress will have NO LIMITS. I am not limited by the limitations of this present world. I am born from above, filled with God's Spirit, called according to His purpose, and a recipient of continual divine favor. Therefore, I live with a FORWARD-EVER, BACKWARD-NEVER mentality. The best is yet to come for me and my household!

SECTION 11

BONUS CONTENT

Declarations of Faith Using the Names of God

Declarations of Faith Using the Names of God

El Shaddai: (Gen 35:11,12)

• You are my All-Sufficient One!

• I do not need to seek out any other gods; my sufficiency is in You!

• I have no worry, no doubt, and no fear; because El Shaddai is with me today and every day.

• My faith is in You and You alone, God!

• You are my source and my supply!

• I am Abraham's seed and an heir according to the covenant promises.

El Elyon: (Gen 14:18-20)

• You are the Most-High God!

• I succeed in every endeavor, even against ridiculous odds, because the Most-High God is with me!

• You have given me the wisdom to devise the proper plan of attack.

• You have given me the power to get wealth.

• You have given me the blueprint for victory.

• I receive the victory and praise You – El Elyon – for it in advance!

Adonai: (Isaiah 6:8)

- Adonai, You are the Lord of all in my life!

- You sit on the throne and are worthy to be praised!

- I am cleansed from sin and guilt by Your touch and Your blood.

- I serve You today with a clean heart and a pure spirit.

- You are my Master, and I am your servant.

- You are also my Father, and I am your child.

- So I walk with the boldness of a child and the submission of a servant!

- I am available to You, Father, for You are my LORD!

Jehovah: (Ex 3:14)

• Lord Jehovah, I praise You!

• You are the God that defines Himself by Himself!

• You are the God of the already (my past).

• You are the God of the right now (my present).

• And you are the God of the not yet (my future).

• You know the thoughts I have before I think them.

• You know the concerns I have before I feel them.

• And You know the plans You have for me before I learn them.

• I can face anything this day has for me because You – Jehovah – are with me!

Jehovah-Nissi: (Ex 17:15)

• Jehovah-Nissi, You are my Banner and My Battle-Ax!

• I fight under Your flag.

• I defend Your precepts, principles, and ways.

• I submit myself to Your Word and Your commandments.

• By my obedience to Your Word, I cause my way to be prosperous today.

• I do Your work, Your way, and receive Your results.

• No enemy shall overtake me because I am a soldier in Your Army, Father.

Jehovah-Rohi: (Psalm 23)

• Jehovah-Rohi, You are my shepherd, and I shall not want!

• You lead me toward peaceful places.

• You minister to my every need.

• You have my best interest in Your heart.

• You prepare a table for me in the presence of all my enemies.

• You promote me in front of my haters, causing them to be spectators of my success.

• I will fear no evil because You are with me, even in the valley of the shadow of death!

• You anoint me afresh for this day and every day.

• I walk in Your benefits and enjoy Your protection.

• Surely goodness and mercy shall pursue me all the days of my life!

Jehovah-Rapha: (Exodus 15:26)

- Lord God, You are my Healer!
- I submit and surrender myself to your Word and Your voice.
- I walk in obedience to You, and You keep me in perfect health.
- I take the healing Jesus died to give me, and I release most holy faith to bring these things to pass.
- I declare that my body will function in perfection!
- Every sickness, germ, or disease that attempts to hinder my body must die instantly!
- I live a divine life, and I live in divine health!
- Because you live in me, yokes are destroyed, and burdens are removed in my life!

Jehovah-Shammah: (Eze 48:35)

• You are my Jehovah Shammah, my ever-present help in the time of trouble!

• You are here with me today and will always be with me!

• You keep me through every situation and bless me in the midst of my enemies.

• Your presence brings with it Your Power, Your Protection, and Your Peace!

• You are with me everywhere I go, and You cause my way to prosper!

Jehovah-Tsidkenu: (Jer 23:6)

• You are my righteousness!

• You have delivered me from the guilt of sin and cleansed me by the washing of Your Word.

• I am restored to the right relationship with You.

• I can do what You say I can do!

• I can have what You say I can have!

• I am not a sinner; I am a child of God!

• I am not wrong with You; Jesus has made me Right!

• I can now face anything that comes my way with Freedom, Liberty, and Power!

Jehovah-Shalom: (Jud 6:24)

• You are my Peace, Father!

• You are bigger than anything that will ever come my way.

• You enable me to accomplish every task with excellence and in victory.

• I have Your peace, even in seemingly impossible circumstances.

• I can do all things through Christ today and every day.

• I cast down fear and doubt, and I walk in Your perfect peace and Your perfect power!

• I have peace on the inside, even when things are going haywire on the outside.

• I am not moved by external circumstances.

• I am strong, stable, and secure!

Jehovah-M'kaddesh: (Lev 20:8)

• You are the God that sets me apart!

• I am different from the world.

• I am set apart, and I am comfortable with it.

• I do not act like the world; I am holy because my God is holy.

• I live under a different set of laws.

• I am your child, and I act it everywhere I go.

• I will stay focused and dedicated to pleasing You!

• I will love You with all my heart and also love my neighbors as myself.

• I will submit myself to the leadership of the Holy Spirit!

• I will walk in accordance with your Word!

• I will live as a set-apart one today and every day!

Jehovah-Jireh: (Genesis 22:14)

• You are my Provider, Lord!

• I put nothing nor anyone above You!

• You are my Righteous King and my Everlasting Ruler!

• I submit and surrender to You, and You alone.

• I walk by faith and not by sight.

• I trust You, Father, even when I cannot see nor totally understand what You are doing.

• I know that you will provide all my needs according to Your riches in glory.

• I obey Your commandments, and I enjoy Your provision.

• All my bills are paid, all the time, on time! I attack my lack.

• You have given me the power to get wealth.

• I am provided for today and every day because I serve the Great Provider!

Jehovah-Sabaoth: (1 Samuel 1:3)

- You are my ultimate authority!
- You are bigger than every situation and stronger than any opposition!
- Every obstacle in my path is but a small thing to You.
- I submit and surrender myself to You this day.
- I, like Hannah, make a vow to serve you all the days of my life and place my every desire at Your feet.
- I am a soldier in Your Army, and I obey Your commands.
- Use me this day for Your service.
- I am present for duty and fit to fight!

El Olam: (Isaiah 26:4)

• You are my Everlasting King!

• I trust you today and every day, even in the midst of an ever-changing and often frustrating environment.

• I trust you with my life, family, finances, career, and decisions!

• You know what plans You have for me; plans to prosper me and not to harm me; plans to give me an expected end!

• As my everlasting God, I submit and surrender myself to You and to those plans.

• I thank You for where I am and trust You to take me to where I need to be!

El Gibhor: (Psalm 24:8)

- You are the King of Glory! You are my Mighty God!
- You never sleep and are always armed and battle-ready.
- You have the greatest Quick Reaction Force (QRF) anywhere.
- You have a heavenly host of angels always on duty, ready to come to my aid.
- I have repented of my sin and have a blood-bought right to Your protection.
- I enter into this day with your angels encamped around me!
- I am safe because You make me safe. I enjoy divine protection.
- I can face any obstacle and any opposition because You, Mighty God, will fight for me!
- The battle is not mine, but Yours!

El Roi: (Gen 16:13)

• You are the God who sees me in every situation!

• Even when I place myself in the wilderness and find myself by myself, You see me and are there.

• Your Sight brings with it Your visitation.

• Your visitation brings with it Your vision.

• Your vision brings with it Your Provision!

• I can see because You see me!

• I can face this day because You see me!

• I can accomplish every task and overcome every hindrance because You – El Roi – See me!

• I am never hopeless because I am never helpless!

• I am seen, loved, and cared for as Your child!

Elohim: (Gen 1:1)

- You are my creator, God!

- Your words have creative ability.

- I am created in Your image and after your likeness.

- My words, lined up with Your Word, have creative ability!

- I speak to every chaotic situation in my life and pronounce order!

- I speak to every unruly area of my life and pronounce peace!

- My family is blessed. My children are blessed. My household is blessed!

- My finances are blessed. My workplace is blessed! My businesses are blessed!

- My hands are blessed, and whatever I put my hands to do, prospers because You, God –

Elohim are with me!

*** Lord, be it unto me, according to Thy Word and my declaration of faith!

I declare all these things in JESUS' name, and I believe I receive. Amen.

CONCLUSION

We only get one shot at life. God planned for our arrival before the world began, He brought us into the world at just the right time, and we then get to attempt to make the most of the life He gave us. I hope you can see, by going through this book, that your words matter. The more you train yourself to think, act, and speak like God on the earth, the more heaven will be manifested in your life.

Part of my purpose in life is to help others discover theirs. In these pages, I have provided you with words that will help condition your heart to hear God's voice and follow His Spirit. I pray this book blessed you. Here is my prayer for you:

May the Lord use you within your sphere of influence to accomplish His Kingdom plans and purposes while you are in the land of the living.

ABOUT THE AUTHOR

Rick Piña has been preaching the Gospel of Jesus the Christ for over 26 years. His daily devotional, Today's Word, has been impacting lives all over the world for over 25 years. Part of Rick's purpose in life is to help others discover their purpose and complete it before they die. He preaches a message of faith, hope, and grace.

Rick and his wife, Isabella, lead Rick and Isabella Piña Ministries (RIPMinistries). They oversee a church in the Dominican Republic (Grace Destiny Church) and a school (the Thelma Steward Destiny Academy). The ministry provides a Christ-based education to disadvantaged children, training them to become the men/women God called them to be.

Born in Brooklyn to immigrant parents and raised in a multiracial environment, Rick easily connects with all people, of all backgrounds, at all levels. Like Paul, God has graced Rick to become all things to all people so that through the grace of God on his life, some may be saved.

Rick is also an accomplished technologist with over 30 years of experience in the information technology field. He retired from the United States Army in 2015, after serving his nation for 25 years. His culminating assignment was serving as the United States Army Chief Technology Officer (CTO) and Principal Technical Advisor to the Army Chief Information Officer (CIO).

Rick is a sought-after thought leader in the IT/Cybersecurity field. He clearly articulates the connection between emerging technology and organizational gaps and requirements.

Rick serves on multiple non-profit boards, and he is very active in efforts to advance Diversity and Inclusion. He holds an M.B.A. and a Bachelor of Science Degree in Business Administration from Trident University. He is also a Distinguished Member of the U.S. Army Signal Regiment and a recipient of the Signal Corps Regimental Association's Silver Order of Mercury award.

Contact Information

Non-profit organization:
Rick & Isabella Pina Ministries
5501 Merchants View Square, Suite 187
Haymarket, VA 20169
ripministries.org
1-855-JESUS-NOW

Blog:
todaysword.org

Printed materials:
rickpina.co

Apparel and merchandise:
thegracelife.co

YouTube:
/rickpina

Twitter:
@rickpina

Instagram:
@rickpina

Facebook:
/rickpinaofficial

LinkedIn:
/in/rickpinaoffical

Made in United States
Orlando, FL
19 December 2024

56163465R00059